Fannie Lou Hamer

This Little Light of Mine

by Barbara Diamond

Zaner-Bloser
Columbus, Ohio

Table of Contents

Introduction 3

Chapter 1: A Sharecropper's Childhood. 4

Chapter 2: Fannie Lou Marries Pap 11

Chapter 3: Registering to Vote. 15

Chapter 4: Speaking Out. 22

Chapter 5: Fannie Lou Is on National Television . . .26

Chapter 6:
   Fannie Lou Goes to Africa
   and Washington, D.C.. .32

Chapter 7: Fannie Lou Marches 35

Chapter 8: Applause for Fannie Lou 40

Chapter 9: Feeding the Poor. 44

Glossary. 47

Index. 48

Introduction

Fannie Lou Hamer was an unusual and brave woman. In the 1960s and 1970s, she fought for the rights of people in Mississippi and around the world. She fought for people to be able to vote. She fought for people to be educated. She fought so people would have adequate medical care, food, housing, and clothing.

Many times, Fannie Lou stood up for these rights even though she was beaten, fired from her job, and forced out of her home. Her husband Pap and her two daughters stood by her in all her struggles.

Fannie Lou told stories about what happened to her and her family when she tried to register to vote for the first time. She told stories about what happened to her and her friends after they tried to have breakfast and use the bathroom in a **segregated** bus station in Mississippi. When she spoke at the 1964 Democratic National Convention, it was shown on national television. Fannie Lou touched the hearts of people all around the country.

Fannie Lou showed what one person could accomplish in the struggle for freedom and justice.

CHAPTER 1

A Sharecropper's Childhood

Fannie Lou was born on October 6, 1917, in Montgomery County, Mississippi. She was the 20th child born to Lou Ella and Jim Townsend. Her family were **sharecroppers.** They worked in the cotton fields from "can see to can't see," which meant from sunup to sundown. The land belonged to the **plantation** owner who took half their crop. That's why it was called sharecropping, because they had to share their crop.

Slavery had ended over 50 years before Fannie Lou was born. Yet her life and the lives of other sharecroppers in Mississippi were not much better than the slaves' lives had been. Sharecroppers still picked cotton, as the slaves had done. They were still poor and had poor living conditions. They had very little education and not much of a chance to improve their lives.

This girl is picking cotton.

They bought all their supplies from the plantation store and paid for them out of their share of the crop. They were often charged too much and were cheated at the store. If they complained, they risked losing their jobs and income. Since they were often in **debt** to the store and the plantation owner, they could not afford to leave the plantation.

Sharecroppers, including Fannie Lou and her family, usually slept on a cotton sack stuffed with dry grass. Their home was a shack papered with tar. Even though they worked on the land, they were often hungry. Even though they grew cotton, they often could not afford to buy new cotton clothes.

Fannie Lou often told a story about how the plantation boss tricked her into picking cotton at an early age. When she was only six years old, he promised her treats from his store. Her family could rarely afford to buy her treats. She would have to pick 30 pounds of cotton in one week to get the treats. Then this often hungry little girl could have sardines, cheese, and a gingerbread cookie. Even though she had a limp from the time she had **polio,** she managed to pick the 30 pounds.

From then on, little Fannie Lou picked cotton for long hours with her family. She didn't realize until she was older how this boss had tricked her. Of course, she never got those treats for picking cotton again. The next week she was given a bigger sack. She picked sixty pounds, but she didn't get any treats. When she was a teenager picking 200 to 400 pounds of cotton every day, she was paid $1 for her labor.

Sharecropper's children went to school from December to March, because of the planting and picking schedule. Schools were segregated in the South. This meant that African American children went to separate schools from white children. Also, their schools were usually poorly equipped. Fannie Lou loved school. She was very good at spelling and reciting poetry.

When Fannie Lou was 12 years old, she had to stop going to school even during those few months. Her family had managed to save some money because there were 22 members of her family working in the cotton fields. Also, her parents worked extra jobs. Her mother did laundry for the plantation owner's family. Her father served as a Baptist minister. They saved enough money to move off the plantation.

With the money that they had worked so hard to save, her father rented land and bought three mules and two cows. They could now raise their own food. They hoped to finally improve their lives. Fannie Lou loved the animals. She and her brothers and sisters would squirt the cow's milk right into their mouths whenever they were hungry.

One night, though, a white neighbor snuck onto their land and put poison in their animals' feeding trough. It killed all the animals. Her family couldn't support themselves without their animals. They had to move back to the plantation. Many of the white neighbors did not want to see the African American sharecroppers "get somewhere." They wanted to keep things as they were and had been in Mississippi.

For one thing, plantation owners needed cheap labor. Many owners were members of a secret group called the Ku Klux Klan (KKK). This group started after the Civil War to keep African Americans "in their place." Members of the KKK wore white robes and hoods so they could hide who they were. They scared African Americans by burning big crosses on their lawns. They set fire to their houses and churches, beat them, and even killed them. African Americans of the Deep South were afraid of the Klan and other such organizations.

When her family moved back to the plantation, Fannie Lou had to quit school to help her family support themselves. It was then that she joined the Stranger's Home Baptist Church. There she read the Bible with other people and sang hymns and spirituals, which she loved. One of her favorite songs was "This Little Light of Mine." Her faith gave her courage during hard times.

And times were hard for her family, especially during the Great Depression. Often all they had to eat for dinner were **greens** without seasoning and flour gravy, or bread and onions.

Lou Ella, Fannie Lou's mother, was a strong, courageous woman. She didn't let anyone, not even a plantation boss, hurt one of her children. Fannie Lou looked up to her mother. Her mother taught Fannie Lou to respect herself. At one point, Fannie Lou asked her mother why she wasn't white so that they could have some food. Her mother told her, "Don't ever, ever say that again. Don't feel like that. We are not bad because we're black people. You respect yourself as a black child. And when you're grown, if I'm dead and gone, you respect yourself as a black woman, and other people will respect you."

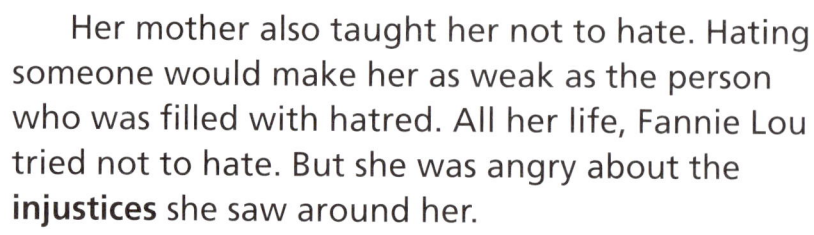

Her mother also taught her not to hate. Hating someone would make her as weak as the person who was filled with hatred. All her life, Fannie Lou tried not to hate. But she was angry about the **injustices** she saw around her.

Even as a teenager, Fannie Lou spoke out about the unfair conditions of African Americans in the South. Her own experiences, her mother's example, and her own strong character gave her the courage to do so.

"I asked God to give me a chance to just let me do something about what was going on in Mississippi," she said. Even as a young woman, Fannie Lou wanted to do what she could to make change. She wanted to make things better for the poor, both African American and white.

CHAPTER 2

Fannie Lou Marries Pap

When Fannie Lou was about 27 years old, she married Perry "Pap" Hamer. For 12 years Pap had worked on the Marlow plantation in Ruleville, Mississippi. He was a tractor driver and farmer.

The Marlows gave them a small shack to live in. It didn't have running water or an indoor toilet. They had to use an outhouse. Working for the Marlows, they earned less than $4 a day.

After a while, Mr. Marlow saw that Fannie Lou was a hard worker. He also noticed that she was smart with numbers. He made her a timekeeper. Her job was to record the number of hours each person on the plantation worked. She kept track of how many bales of cotton they picked and the amount of pay each one should get. She continued working in the fields. At night she cleaned house for the Marlows to earn extra money.

Whenever Fannie Lou could, she tried to make things fairer for her fellow sharecroppers. She believed Mr. Marlow's weighing instruments were not correct. She thought that he cheated his workers. She would take her own weights to work with her. She used them if Mr. Marlow was not nearby.

Fannie Lou and Pap moved to a better house on the Marlow plantation after a while. It had cold running water and a bathroom with a tub and toilet inside. However, the toilet didn't work. So they still had to use an outhouse. One time, when Fannie Lou was cleaning the Marlows' house, Mr. Marlow's daughter said that Fannie Lou didn't have to clean one of the bathrooms very well. It was their dog Honey's bathroom.

Fannie Lou was angry. "Now they got they dog higher 'n us," she told Pap.

This man is drinking at the "colored" water cooler.

Other workers heard Fannie Lou complain about the poor living conditions they all suffered. They warned her she should be careful about what she said. Most African Americans in the Deep South, especially in Mississippi, were afraid to speak out. They all knew of other African Americans who had been beaten or killed for "not keeping their place."

One event happened in 1955, not far from Ruleville where Fannie Lou lived. A boy from Chicago, Emmett Till, came to visit his great uncle. Emmett was 14 years old. He dared to speak to a white woman. For that, he was kidnapped and killed. Later at a trial, his great-uncle bravely pointed out the two men who had taken Emmett from his home. However, an all-white jury found these men not guilty. Later, the two men told a newspaper reporter that they had killed the boy. But they had no fear of ever being jailed for the murder. That was the way things were in Mississippi in 1955.

Fannie Lou and all the other African Americans in Ruleville knew about what happened to Emmett Till. They knew what happened to African Americans who broke the southern rules of segregation. These rules were called the Jim Crow laws. These laws included making African Americans use only the bathrooms and drinking fountains set aside for them. African Americans could not eat at a lunch counter that was for whites only. They had to sit in the back of buses.

Even though others warned Fannie Lou, they respected her for speaking out. They also respected her for trying to be fair as a plantation timekeeper. For extra money, she sold insurance. This made her even more widely known and respected in her community. Her fellow workers knew Fannie Lou worked hard. They knew that what she spoke was true.

Fannie Lou and Pap didn't have any children of their own, so in 1954 they adopted two girls. Dorothy Jean was nine years old and Virgie Ree was five months old when they came to live with them.

Fannie Lou and Pap continued to work hard. Later, Fannie Lou told a magazine, "Sometimes I be working in the fields and I get so tired. I say to the people picking cotton with us, hard as we have to work for nothing, there must be some way we can change this."

By 1962, when Fannie Lou was 44 years old, she found that way.

Chapter 3

Registering to Vote

In 1962, James Bevel and James Forman came to Fannie Lou's town of Ruleville. They called a meeting at the Williamsburg Missionary Baptist Church. They wanted to encourage people there to register to vote.

James Bevel was a member of Martin Luther King Jr.'s group. It was called the Southern Christian Leadership Conference (SCLC). James Forman was from the Student Nonviolent Coordinating Committee (SNCC). These and other groups were involved in the **civil rights** movement in the South. They were trying to help African Americans gain their civil rights. These included the right to vote and the rights to a good education and medical care.

All of these rights were important. But many people in the movement felt that if African Americans couldn't vote, then they wouldn't be able to elect leaders to represent them. It would be very hard for anything to change for African Americans if they couldn't elect people who cared about their civil rights.

Change for African Americans was something most white people in the South did not want. They wanted things to stay the same. They wanted to hold on to their control and power.

Fannie Lou was one of the local people who went to this meeting called by Bevel and Forman. She said later, "I had never heard the freedom songs before! . . . They really wanted to change the world I knew—they wanted Blacks to register to vote!"

She also said that up until that meeting she hadn't realized that African Americans were allowed to vote! She learned about the 15th **Amendment** to the United States **Constitution.** It guaranteed the right to vote regardless of "race, color, or previous condition of servitude."

Fannie Lou decided she wanted the power to vote certain people out of office who made life very hard for her and her neighbors. She also wanted to vote against people like a certain local policeman. His brother had been one of the men who killed 14-year-old Emmett Till.

FANNIE LOU HAMER QUOTE

"There is one thing you have got to learn about our movement. Three people are better than no people."

Fannie Lou said, "That's somethin' I really want to be involved in . . . the only thing they could do to me was kill me, and it seemed like they'd been trying to do that a little bit at a time every since I could remember."

    Along with 17 other people, Fannie Lou signed up to go to Sunflower County in Indianola, Mississippi, to register to vote. A few days later, they got on a bus with two people from the civil rights movement, Robert Moses and Charles McLaurin, to travel the 26 miles.

    The speakers from SNCC and SCLC had warned Fannie Lou and the others that it would be dangerous. They told them what to expect at the courthouse in Indianola. They all knew that they might lose their jobs. They might even be killed just for trying to register to vote. Even with these warnings, they were shocked by what they saw when they arrived at the courthouse.

    There was a crowd of police and white people with guns and dogs in front of the courthouse. The group from Ruleville was frightened. But they were determined to go inside. When they marched to the courthouse, Fannie Lou was the one who led them.

Charles McLaurin later said, "Everybody on the bus was shaking in fear . . . then this voice singing church songs just came out of the crowd and began to calm everybody . . . Somebody said, 'That's Fannie Lou, she know how to sing.'"

The clerk at the courthouse made them come in two at a time to register. Men with rifles walked in and out of the room where voters had to take a literacy test. In Mississippi and other parts of the South, there were many requirements for voting. These made it hard for African Americans to register to vote. The literacy test was one of these. Clerks made the literacy test very hard for African Americans. They didn't want African Americans to be able to pass it. In 1960, Fannie Lou lived in Sunflower County. African Americans were 61% of the voting age population in the county. But they were only 1.2% of registered voters.

There was another way people were scared away from registering to vote. All of their information, such as their name, address, and where they worked, was passed on to the White Citizen's Council. This was a group that made sure African Americans stayed right where they were, poor and overworked, without the rights that would help them improve their conditions.

But Fannie Lou and the others who came to Indianola braved the police and the men with guns. Two by two they went in to register and take the test. Fannie Lou and all the other 17 people from Ruleville failed the literacy test that day. But Fannie Lou was determined. She would come back again and again until she passed.

At the end of the long day, they boarded the bus to go home. But they didn't make it very far. They were stopped at a bridge near Indianola by a state highway patrolman and the local police. When the police arrested two people, all the rest decided it would be better for them to stick together. So they all went back to Indianola. Spirits were low, so Fannie Lou started to sing songs such as "Down by the Riverside" and "This Little Light of Mine." Soon everyone was singing and feeling better.

Finally, after much bargaining, they paid a fine and got into the bus to go home. They were glad they had stuck together. It was harder for the police to put a whole group in jail.

Before Fannie Lou arrived back in Ruleville, word about her trying to register to vote reached her angry employer. Mr. Marlow told Pap that she had to take her name off the **registration** form or leave the plantation.

Mr. Marlow came back to talk to Fannie Lou later. "We're not going to have this in Mississippi," he told her.

Fannie Lou was angry. She had worked so hard for Mr. Marlow for 18 years. She had worked in his fields. She had done the timekeeping, cleaned his house, and cared for his family. And here he was ready to kick her out just because she wanted to vote and improve her life.

Once again, Fannie Lou bravely spoke up. "I didn't go down to Indianola to register for you. I went down there to register for myself."

Pap and Fannie Lou decided together that she should leave. Pap would stay, because Mr. Marlow had threatened to throw away their furniture and fire Pap if he left, too.

Fannie Lou tried to stay with friends in Ruleville. But men with guns shot into the houses of people there who tried to help African Americans register to vote. So she stayed 40 miles away at her niece's house for a while. By December 1962, both Fannie Lou and Pap had lost their jobs and their home. They had no furniture or money. And Fannie Lou had been shot at—all because she wanted to vote.

They decided to move back to Ruleville and stop trying to run from the people who tried to scare them. Fannie Lou felt she had done nothing wrong, so there was no need for her to run away. Cars full of white men with guns continued to drive past their house and follow Fannie Lou and her family when they walked in the streets. The men called them names and threatened them. But Fannie Lou and her family stood their ground.

Other people in Ruleville stopped going to the voter registration meetings because they were so frightened by the guns and threats. But not Fanny Lou. She became even more determined. So when Charles McLaurin from SNCC asked Fannie Lou if she would become a local leader in this fight for the right to vote, she said yes. She also agreed to speak at an SNCC rally in Nashville, Tennessee.

CHAPTER 4

Speaking Out

Fannie Lou was a powerful speaker at the Nashville rally. She talked about her dream to the African American and white student volunteers there. Many of them had come from northern cities to help. She told them not to hate the people who were doing these terrible things. Instead, she told them to work hard for change. She asked them to tell all their friends in the North to become involved in the civil rights movement. She asked them to contribute money to it. Fannie Lou held everyone's attention with her heartfelt story.

She began to travel around the country with SNCC's Freedom Singers. One person said that Mrs. Hamer "set her listeners afire."

She came back to Ruleville and worked hard talking to people, urging them to register. The local people respected her. They began to work again with the SNCC workers, even though it was dangerous. Fannie Lou became an SNCC field secretary. She helped get free food and clothing for the poor. She encouraged people to register to vote.

Sometimes she traveled, speaking out, singing, and raising money to support the civil rights cause. All over the United States, Fannie Lou talked about how hard it was for African Americans in Mississippi and their hopes for change.

On December 4, 1962, Fannie Lou went back to Indianola. She tried for a second time to register to vote. Once again, she didn't pass. But she told the clerk, "You'll see me every 30 days until I pass." Later she told people, "There was nothing they could take from me any longer."

On June 10, 1963, on her third try, Fannie Lou finally passed. There were 30,000 African Americans in Sunflower County. She became the first one to register to vote. That was a proud day for Fannie Lou Hamer. She and her family continued to live with threatening letters and phone calls. They even had carloads of men with guns driving around their house. Even so, Fannie Lou and her family were determined to fight for their rights.

In the spring of 1963, Fannie Lou traveled to Charleston, South Carolina. She and the other people were going for more voter education training. Their bus trip home was one of the most terrifying experiences for Fannie Lou and all the others.

As their bus arrived at a rest stop in Winona, Mississippi, four members of her group got off the bus to buy food at the bus terminal. Two more got off to use the restrooms. This was still a time when African Americans could not use the lunchrooms and bathrooms in bus stations because they were for whites only. They had to look for "colored only" signs or do without. The chief of police and state highway patrolman ordered them out of the terminal. They put the six in a police car. Fannie Lou got off the bus and they arrested her, too.

The police took Fannie Lou and the others to the Montgomery County jail. There, the police severely beat them. Word that they were in jail and being abused reached the SNCC and SCLC offices. Andrew Young, James Bevel, and Dorothy Cotton came from these organizations to the jail to help Fannie Lou and the others. They managed to arrange for their release with the help of the federal government. They carried Fannie Lou and the others out of the jail and took them for medical help.

Fannie Lou stayed in Atlanta for a month to heal. She had to miss hearing Martin Luther King Jr. give his famous "I Have a Dream" speech in Washington, D.C.

The beating had a permanent physical effect on Fannie Lou. Her limp from polio grew worse. She couldn't see out of her left eye. Her kidneys were damaged.

Fannie Lou Hamer marched in a voter-registration demonstration in 1963.

But this beating did not damage Fannie Lou's resolve to fight for the right to vote for African Americans in the South. She knew that without the right to vote, African Americans would not have control over their lives. As soon as she could, she went back to Ruleville and talked to people. She encouraged them to register to vote. In the cotton fields and in the churches, she talked about the importance of voting. And she sang the freedom songs she loved.

It seemed that the harder the people in power made it for Fannie Lou, the harder she fought back. "With all that my parents and grandparents gave to Mississippi, I have a right to stay here and fight for what they didn't get," she said.

CHAPTER 5

Fannie Lou Is on National Television

Fannie Lou kept on fighting. In August 1963, even though she was registered to vote, Fannie Lou found out she couldn't. She hadn't paid the poll tax. This tax on voting was another way African Americans were kept from voting. Many were too poor to pay the tax. African Americans were 40% of Mississippi's population by this time, or almost one million people. But only 28,000 African Americans were registered voters. On the other hand, 95% of the 1 ¼ million white people were registered.

The civil rights movement made progress. On January 23, 1964, the 24th Amendment to the U.S. Constitution passed. This amendment outlawed the poll tax.

Many people in power in Mississippi said that African Americans didn't care about voting. They said that was why so few of them were registered. What really happened was that African Americans tried to vote. And they tried to be part of the regular **Democratic Party.** If they tried to attend a party meeting, they found the doors locked or the place the meeting was held was kept secret.

Given the chance, African Americans would vote. Fannie Lou and other people in the civil rights organizations had to prove this. They knew these people only needed the opportunity to vote.

They started a new party called the Mississippi Freedom Democratic Party, or MFDP, in May 1964. They planned a Freedom Election. Even though the election wouldn't actually count, it would show that African Americans did care.

SNCC, SCLC, and the other civil rights groups organized Freedom Summer. Hundreds of volunteers, including many from the North, came to Mississippi. They helped to start Freedom Schools. The Freedom Schools taught reading, citizenship, and African American history, and provided instruction on registering to vote.

Fannie Lou and several other African Americans decided to run for office. She went all around the state meeting people. She told them how important it was to vote. She told them it was important to elect African Americans to all offices. They needed representatives in the local, state, and federal governments. That way, they could start to have some say over their own lives. Fannie Lou ran against James Whitten. He had been a Mississippi congressman for over 20 years.

The summer of 1964 was a very busy one for Fannie Lou. Her home became the headquarters for the 30 campaign volunteers. The volunteers came from all over the country. Her husband Pap agreed with Fannie Lou. He knew that this was an important way to fight for their rights, even though it meant losing their jobs.

Fannie Lou also took charge of food and clothing drives for the poor. Thousands of pounds of donations came from all over. Fannie Lou distributed everything. She always reminded people to register to vote as she handed them dresses and shoes, and dried milk and cheese.

By August 1964, the MFDP had their election. Over 60,000 people "voted." Most of them still were not registered to vote in the actual elections. Voting places were set up in churches and beauty parlors and even on the streets. The MFDP encouraged everyone to vote, whites and African Americans.

Sixty-eight MFDP delegates were elected. They would go to the Democratic Party's national convention in Atlantic City. There they hoped to help choose the Democratic candidate. He would run for president of the United States. Sixty-four of the MFDP's delegates were African American. Four were white. Fannie Lou was elected a delegate and the vice chair.

After a 1200-mile bus ride, the MFDP delegates arrived in Atlantic City on August 21. They had high hopes. They wanted to "be seated." This would mean they could vote on issues and candidates at the convention. They were prepared to tell the special committee that they had the right to be seated. The committee was called the Credentials Committee. They believed the regular delegates from the all-white Mississippi Democratic Party didn't have that right. They said the regular delegates didn't represent all the people of their state. They were prepared to tell the committee the truth about voting in Mississippi. They would say it wasn't fair and that African Americans were kept from voting.

FANNIE LOU HAMER QUOTE

"Nobody's free until everybody's free."

Members of each group had to speak before the Credentials Committee. Each speaker was allowed eight minutes to talk. The hearing was on national television. These speakers spoke not only in front of the committee, but the whole country.

Fannie Lou's speech stirred up the whole nation. She spoke about what had happened to her and Pap when she tried to register to vote in Indianola. She told them about being beaten in the jail in Winona. She ended her speech with these words: "If the Freedom Democratic Party is not seated now, I question America. Is this America, the land of the free and the home of the brave, where we have to sleep with our telephones off of the hook because our lives be threatened daily, because we want to live as decent human beings in America?"

The next day, many people who had heard Fannie Lou speak on television sent telegrams to their delegates. They told their delegates they supported the new party from Mississippi. In the end, though, the Credentials Committee did not vote in favor of the MFDP delegates. The Credentials Committee did not allow them to "be seated" at the convention. They said only two could sit and watch. But they couldn't vote. The committee made a promise, however. At the next convention, in 1968, they would not allow an all-white delegation to be seated.

Fannie Lou Hamer testified before the Credentials Committee in 1964.

The MFDP delegates were very disappointed. They left the convention. Most of the regular white Mississippi Democrats left, too. They did not like the fact that they would have to include African Americans in their future delegations to the National Democratic Conventions.

One thing was certain. After hearing Fannie Lou on television, many more Americans now knew what it was really like for African Americans who tried to vote in the South. Many more Americans became sympathetic to their cause.

CHAPTER 6

Fannie Lou Goes to Africa and Washington, D.C.

After the convention, the MFDP delegates were tired. A famous African American singer named Harry Belafonte saw that they needed a vacation. Eleven of the delegates were chosen to go with him to Africa. Fannie Lou was one of them. She had never been out of the United States before.

Because Harry Belafonte knew the president of Guinea, they traveled there. They were treated with great respect by President Toure. Fannie Lou was amazed to see black pilots and flight attendants on the plane that took them to Guinea. And she was amazed that President Toure came to see them himself.

As she traveled around Guinea, Fannie Lou heard songs that reminded her of the ones her slave grandmother used to sing. She saw women carrying heavy containers of water on their heads. This reminded her of her mother who did the same in Mississippi. For the first time, she saw the connections between African Americans and their roots in Africa.

"I cried over there," she said. "I probably got relatives right now in Africa, but we'll never know each other because we've been separated . . . I'll never know them and they'll never know me."

Her trip proved to her that "it is there within us. We can do things if we only get the chance."

The trip to Africa lasted three weeks. Fannie Lou returned to Mississippi more relaxed and changed by her experience. She was ready to continue the fight for freedom.

Fannie Lou and two other African American women decided to run for office. The other women were Annie Devine and Victoria Gray. They decided to run for the U.S. House of Representatives. The women challenged three Mississippi congressmen in the fall election. Fannie Lou still believed the biggest fight was for the right to vote. She wanted people to elect leaders who really represented the people in their district.

Once again, African Americans could not vote in the election. So the MFDP held their own election. In their election, Fannie Lou won over James Whitten. He was the same man she had tried to run against in the June Democratic primary. The June primary election was held to decide who would represent the Democratic Party in the fall election. Now this fall election would decide who would represent Mississippi in the United States Congress.

After this election, the MFDP learned about a rule they could use in the House of Representatives in Washington. The rule would help them challenge the regular Mississippi Democrats when they were about to take their seats as congressmen. To prepare for the challenge, the MFDP's lawyers gathered facts to build their case. Fannie Lou and others traveled the country to raise funds. They talked to representatives from other states. They asked the representatives to support them.

In January 1965, Fannie Lou, Annie Devine, and Victoria Gray all went to Washington. Hundreds were there to support their cause.

Congress voted to seat the regular Mississippi congressmen but not the MFDP candidates. The vote was 276 to 149. But they made the MFDP candidates a promise. They promised there would be an investigation into the voting practices in Mississippi.

The MFDP and their supporters would have to wait to hear what the House Subcommittee on Elections decided. But they didn't just wait. They continued to work, step by step, on their road to voting rights and freedom.

CHAPTER 7

Fannie Lou Marches

In January 1965, Fannie Lou, Victoria, and Annie went to Washington. At the same time, SNCC was organizing marches in Selma, Alabama. The marches were to protest voting injustices. Day after day, African Americans in Selma marched to the courthouse. They were asking for the right to vote. Thousands were arrested, including schoolchildren.

A man was killed by state troopers in a town near Selma. He was trying to protect his mother during a voting rights march. All the civil rights workers in the area were very angry about the killing. Martin Luther King Jr. and his organization planned a 54-mile march. They marched from the city of Selma to Montgomery, the capital of Alabama. They wanted this march to focus national attention on the crisis.

The marchers were led by Hosea Williams and John Lewis. When they reached the bridge at the edge of Selma, state police ran at the marchers with tear gas and beat them. The national television news that night showed what looked like a war in Selma. People all over the United States were horrified by what was happening in the South.

After the bridge incident, people from all over went to Selma to support the marchers. Fannie Lou joined them. She marched with Martin Luther King Jr. and thousands of others. She marched despite her limp from polio and the Winona jail beatings. Martin Luther King Jr. reached Montgomery, Alabama, five days later. By then there were 25,000 people marching behind him.

Marchers crossed the Pettus Bridge in Selma in 1965.

John Lewis said of the march, "It was black people, it was white people, it was Protestant, it was Jewish, and it was Catholic. There were young people, old people, some very poor people, some very rich people . . . People came from all over. They blended together and we all marched together."

The marches in Selma and the many other activities of people such as Fannie Lou worked. They helped convince politicians and President Lyndon Johnson that it was time to do something about the injustices in the South.

On August 6, 1965, President Johnson signed the Voting Rights Act. This was a great victory for Fannie Lou and the other activists. This act set up a system where federal examiners would serve as voter registrars. They would replace the local officials. They would make sure every eligible citizen could vote. It outlawed the literacy test. The poll tax was already gone, having been outlawed by the passing of the 24th Amendment to the Constitution.

During the spring, Fannie Lou and the MFDP were still working on their case in Washington. They wanted to unseat the regular congressmen from Mississippi. In May 1965, the MFDP gave the House of Representatives 3,000 papers. These papers described unfair voting practices in Mississippi. Fannie Lou and others spoke and raised funds to get more support in the months leading up to the decision.

On September 17, 1965, Fannie Lou, Victoria Gray (now Victoria Adams), and Annie Devine were given seats on the House floor. They were there to hear the decision on their case. They were the first African American women ever allowed to do this. That day the gallery of the House of Representatives was packed with people. They had come to hear the decision. There were even people standing outside the Capitol on the streets waiting to hear.

Representative Ryan from New York quoted the Constitution, supporting the challenge to the Mississippi regulars. He said the Constitution provided that "the right of citizens of the United States to vote shall not be denied or abridged by the United States, or by any state, on account of race, color or previous condition of servitude."

The Mississippi regulars said that the three women had not been candidates on the ballot. They said the three women were not qualified to be seated as congressmen. Of course, they did not admit that the three women had tried to get on the ballot and were denied that right. Of the congressmen, 228 voted to dismiss the challenge, 143 voted to uphold it. So the challenge was lost.

Fannie Lou was crying when reporters talked to her after the decision. "I'm not crying for myself alone," she said. "I'm crying for America. Because it's later than you think."

Fannie Lou Hamer spoke to Mississippi Freedom Democratic Party members outside the Capitol in Washington, D.C., in 1965.

    Although Fannie Lou didn't win this challenge, she did see the Voting Rights Act of 1965 pass. Things were changing in Mississippi and all over the South. Southern politicians could no longer stop registration of African Americans. They could no longer take away their right to vote and run for office. What they did do to African Americans was no longer a dark secret. Americans all over the country were now aware of their unjust practices.

    As Fannie Lou said after the defeat of their challenge, "It ain't over yet. We're coming back here, again and again, and again." And people knew that Fannie Lou would, just as she had when registering to vote in Indianola. Fannie Lou was a determined, persistent, powerful voice for freedom.

CHAPTER 8

Applause for Fannie Lou

Fannie Lou Hamer was a woman who did not give up. She continued to fight for the rights of African Americans to register to vote. She continued to fight even after Congress's decision to dismiss their case about unfair elections in Mississippi.

James Meredith had been the first African American to go to the University of Mississippi. In 1966, Meredith decided to lead a march. It would go from Memphis, Tennessee, to Jackson, Mississippi. The march would encourage African Americans to register to vote. He called this the March Against Fear. On June 6, 1966, he was shot and hospitalized. This was the second day of the march. Martin Luther King Jr. led the march after that. He started from the place where Meredith had been shot. Fannie Lou and many others joined him.

For ten days, the march was peaceful. The marchers were able to register many new voters on their way. Mississippi's governor wasn't happy with this. He reduced police protection for the marchers. Then, in Canton, Mississippi, police began to arrest some of the marchers without good reasons. They began to use tear gas on them.

Because of their determination, the marchers kept on going. James Meredith was released from the hospital and joined them. On June 21, 15,000 people heard Martin Luther King Jr. speak. He called this "the greatest demonstration for freedom ever held in the state of Mississippi." Because of this march, almost 4,000 African Americans registered to vote.

In 1967, Fannie Lou's daughter Dorothy became very ill. She had just given birth to her second child. Fannie Lou took her to the two nearest hospitals. But they refused to take care of Dorothy because she was African American. At that time, hospitals were still segregated in Mississippi. Some treated whites, and some treated African Americans. Fannie Lou tried to drive Dorothy to the hospital in Memphis, Tennessee. It was over 100 miles away. But Dorothy never made it. She died in her mother's arms.

Dorothy's death was a very sad time for Fannie Lou and Pap. They took Dorothy's two little girls into their home and raised them.

Dorothy's death and having two very young children to care for slowed Fannie Lou down. But she still continued to work for what she believed in. While speaking in San Francisco in 1967, Fannie Lou raised money for the poor in Mississippi. She said this about the voting problems in her home state: "This is not Mississippi's problem, this is America's problem."

Fannie Lou Hamer spoke to the delegates during the 1968 Democratic Convention.

One of the victories in Fannie Lou's life happened in 1968, not long after her daughter's death. That summer was the Democratic Party's National Convention in Chicago. Fannie Lou's party was the Mississippi Freedom Democratic Party. They had joined with some people from the regular Mississippi Democratic Party.

They formed a new group called the Loyal Democrats of Mississippi, or the Loyalists. Half the people they elected to go to Chicago were white and half were African American. Fannie Lou was one of them. She was elected as a delegate from the district of Winona. This was the same place where she suffered the beatings in jail.

This time was different. Once again they challenged the seating of the regular Mississippi Democratic Party, all of whom were white. This time, they won before the convention's Credentials Committee. The vote was 85 to 9. The regulars would have to leave the convention. The Loyalists, Fannie Lou included, would take their place.

The regulars shouted "illegal" and "unconstitutional." The chairmen, however, pointed to a piece of paper. It was from the 1964 convention. The paper ordered the Mississippi delegation to include African Americans. The Loyalists shouted, "Free at last" and "We shall overcome," as they took their seats. When Fannie Lou took her seat, people all over the convention hall stood up and clapped. She got a standing ovation!

One of the other Mississippi delegates at the convention said that Fannie Lou "was about justice. She was not just about black. She was about justice wherever it came down, and she was able to voice it that way—that it was a matter of justice."

CHAPTER 9

Feeding the Poor

The right to vote was still very important to Fannie Lou. But after the 1968 Democratic National Convention, she put more of her energy into caring for the poor. She said, "If you give a hungry man food, he will eat it. If you give a hungry man land, he will grow his own food."

First, she raised money from people around the country and bought 50 pigs. She set up a pig "bank." A poor family could "borrow" a pregnant female pig. They would return it to the "bank" after the piglets were born. The family kept and raised the piglets. As soon as one of their female pigs became pregnant, they lent it to the next needy family.

Then in 1969, Fannie Lou raised more money. She had enough to buy 40 acres of land and farm machines. She started her Freedom Farm Cooperative. This made real her dream of a farm come true. Now African American and white families could raise food crops. These crops included peas, potatoes, beans, and peanuts. Later she bought another 640 acres.

With the meat that they obtained from their pigs and vegetables that they grew, families could feed themselves. They would not suffer from hunger anymore.

Fannie Lou also worked on improving the living conditions of the families who worked on the farm. They applied for farm mortgages through federal government programs. Soon, 70 homes were built on the Freedom Farm property. Fannie Lou and Pap moved into one of these homes. They lived there for the rest of their lives. Unfortunately, the Freedom Farm Cooperative experienced bad weather conditions and financial problems after about five years. Because of this, Fannie Lou's farm dream did not continue after her death.

Fannie Lou suffered from health problems during the 1970s. She still continued to work hard for her causes. She ran for the Mississippi State Senate in 1971. Over 300 African Americans ran for local and state offices in that year. This was more than ever before. This showed that the work of Fannie Lou and others had been successful.

She lost that election. Afterwards she said, "Ain't nothing going to be handed to you on a silver platter, nothing . . . You've got to fight. Every step of the way, you've got to fight."

Fifty African Americans did win offices in Mississippi. This was the largest number of African Americans elected to office in the South at that time.

Fannie Lou's health continued to grow worse. She died on March 14, 1977. She was almost 60 years of age. Her funeral was held at the very same church where she had first heard about voter registration. So many people came that a second funeral was held at the local high school.

A speaker at the funeral was Andrew Young. He was one of the people who had helped free her from the Winona jail. He said, "The many people who are now elected officials would not be where they are had we not stood up then. And there was not one of those that was not influenced and inspired by the spirit of this one woman, Mrs. Hamer."

It was very appropriate that Mr. Young ended the service. He led everyone in the song Fannie Lou loved, "This Little Light of Mine."

From the Mississippi Delta to the halls of Congress, Fannie Lou was not afraid to speak out. She spoke out for justice and freedom. She let her little light shine for all the world to see.

Glossary

amendment: a change or alteration, especially to a set of laws

civil rights: pertaining to rights to personal freedom established by the 13th and 14th Amendments to the Constitution and established also by other acts of Congress

Constitution: the written set of fundamental principles by which the United States is governed

debt: that which a person owes and is obligated to pay to or perform for another person

Democratic Party: founded in 1828, one of the two major political parties in the United States

greens: leafy plants or plant parts eaten as vegetables

injustices: unjust actions that are a violation of another's rights

plantation: pertaining to a farm especially in tropical or partially tropical climates on which tobacco, cotton, coffee or another crop is raised.

polio: short for poliomyelitis, a disease that can result in paralysis of the spine. It was more common before the discovery of the Salk vaccine.

registration: pertaining to the act of making an entry in an official register, list, or book

segregated: separated or set apart from others, especially because of race

sharecroppers: tenant farmers or people who farm on someone else's land and pay a share of the crop as rent

Index

Bevel, James, 15, 16, 24
Credentials Committee, 29–31, 43
Devine, Annie, 33, 34, 35, 38
Forman, James, 15, 16
Freedom Farm Cooperative, 44-45
Gray, Victoria (later Adams, Victoria), 33, 34, 35, 38
Hamer, Dorothy Jean, 14, 41, 42
Hamer, Perry "Pap," 11, 12, 14, 19, 20, 28, 30, 41, 45
Hamer, Virgie Ree, 14
King, Jr., Martin Luther, 15, 24, 35, 36, 40, 41
Lewis, John, 35, 37
Loyal Democrats of Mississippi, 43
McLaurin, Charles, 17, 18, 21

Meredith, James, 40, 41
Mississippi Freedom Democratic Party (MFDP), 27–34, 37, 39, 42
Moses, Robert, 17
sharecroppers, 4–8, 11
Southern Christian Leadership Conference (SCLC), 15, 17, 24, 27
Student Nonviolent Coordinating Committee (SNCC), 15, 17, 21, 22, 24, 27, 35
Till, Emmett, 13, 16
Townsend, Lou Ella, 4, 7, 9, 10
Voting Rights Act of 1965, 37, 39
Williams, Hosea, 35
Young, Andrew, 24, 46